LIST OF COLOUR ILLUSTRATIONS

FRONT COVER: The Memorial to Thomas Harding at 'Martyrs' Dell', which stands overlooking the Town of Chesham on the slope of White Hill. It marks the site of his execution in 1532, by burning at the stake. *(Photo, Clive Foxell)*

INSIDE FRONT COVER: An exterior view of the south porch of St Mary's Church showing the turret which contains the stairs, leading to the parvise – also known as a 'spirit loft', or priest's room – which occupies the upper floor over the south porch. Tradition has it that Thomas Harding was confined here prior to the day before his execution. *(Photo, Clive Foxell)*

INSIDE REAR COVER: An interior view shows the open door within St Mary's south west wall leading to the turret stair and the parvise. *(Photo, Clive Foxell)*

REAR COVER: The Ionic Cross, which stands in St Mary's Churchyard and was erected in 1907 by the Protestant Alliance, to the memory of Thomas Harding. *(Photo, Clive Foxell)*

FIRST PUBLISHED 1982

SECOND EDITION (Illustrated and Revised) 2010

Published by Clive Foxell
at 4 Meades Lane, Chesham, Bucks, HP5 1ND
clive.foxell@btinternet.com

Any proceeds from the sales of this book will be given to
The Friends of St Mary's

ISBN 978 0 9564178 1 7

Printed by:
Orbitpress Ltd,
11 Market Square,
Chesham,
Bucks, HP5 1HG

Opposite: The writ of 'de heretico comburendo' condemning Thomas Harding to execution.

THE LIFE AND TIMES of

THOMAS HARDING

CHESHAM'S LOLLARD MARTYR

ARNOLD BAINES & SHIRLEY FOXELL

Contents

Preface

It had been in 1982 that the first version of this booklet was published. Dr. Arnold Baines, in his capacity as a senior and most respected figure in local government, representing Chesham at Town Council, Chiltern District, and Bucks County levels, had also been the acknowledged expert in Chesham's local history, and it was he who had recognised the importance of 1982 to the Town's history in that it marked, for Chesham, the 450th anniversary of the execution of Thomas Harding, burnt at the stake for practising the Lollard heresy. The event, a very late manifestation of this ghastly punishment, had been well documented by Foxe, in his Acts & Monuments: so precise dates and sites were known. A notable series of events was planned for Chesham, which included an exhibition of documents, coupled with a flower festival at St Mary's Church; and a project was organised by Thomas Harding School. The original of this booklet was also produced then.

Dr. Baines had expressed the wish that he himself should concentrate on the later, second, part of the story, relating to Harding. So it fell to myself to write the first part, which was to trace the early evolution of Lollardy and how its connection with Chesham had developed. The published booklet was well received and there has since been a steady demand for it, to the extent that, recently, photcopies have been produced to fill the gap.

Against this background, and with the encouragement both of Revd. Simon Cansdale, Rector of Chesham, and The Friends of St Mary's, it has been decided to produce this new version, complete with illustrations.

Sadly, in 2001, Dr Baines died, leaving a gap in so many of Chesham's spheres of activity, not least that of local history. Needless to say, what he wrote in 1982 still stands, and it has been left as he wrote it. The first, earlier Lollard, part of the booklet also remains unaltered from the 1982 version as it stood then. However, the opportunity has been taken to make additions to the Bibliography, including mention of Dr Davies's seminal article, 'Lollardy & Locality'.

In conclusion, sincere thanks and love must go to my husband, Clive, and my daughter, Elizabeth, for all their hard work: to Clive for producing this illustrated format – including his photographs: and to Elizabeth for painstaking checks for typographical errors and spelling inconsistencies. However, any remaining errors are my own responsibility

Shirley Foxell, Chesham, 2010

PART 1:   The Lollards of Chesham

There had been Lollards in England for a hundred and fifty years when Thomas Harding met his cruel death at the stake on that May morning in 1532. Throughout that period the Chilterns had been one of the main strongholds of this, 'the old English heresy'. What was heresy? What indeed were Lollards, and how did they come to exist in the Chilterns and, more especially, in Chesham?

The Medieval Church and Learning

There was no choice of opting out of the medieval Church. It was a compulsory society, the ark of salvation in a sea of destruction. It may have possessed no actual power, and have needed to depend on the goodwill of secular rulers to protect its tenets and fight its battles, but people were nevertheless expected to obey its laws. Those who defied it and offered a threat to its established order were branded as heretics.

But, having said that, there is no doubt that, beneath the seemingly united surface of the Church, there existed a lively mixture of popular religion made up of many different elements borrowed from ancient folk cults which, as the centuries progressed, became blended with Church doctrine. And on an intellectual level too there was certainly room to manoeuvre. But, given the broadness of the medieval Church, and accepting the inevitability of deviation within its mighty boundary, nevertheless the dividing line between orthodoxy and heterodoxy was a very fine one, and from time to time heresy did rear its ugly head. And, whereas in the early days of the Church, the battles were mostly of words, later, as it became temporally more powerful and had 'more to lose', then blood was to flow and flesh was to burn in the cause of the true faith.

Twelfth century Europe witnessed, within the new universities, a flowering of art and learning. Scholars would travel the length and breadth of the Continent in search of the great teachers, and many of these enquiring minds were to set their mark on Christian doctrine. The culmination of this renaissance was reached in the life and work of St Thomas Aquinas. Using the rediscovered works of the Greek philosophers, especially those of Aristotle, Aquinas created a vast edifice of doctrine around the central problem of faith and reason. He argued that reason and revelation are compatible. Far from dismissing the sensible world as an unreal shadow, as some philosophers, notably Plato, had done, Aquinas demonstrated that here lay the surest evidence of reality. But Aquinas represented the intellectual calm before the storm. By the time the Middle Ages had ended, faith and reason, or in other words, theology and philosophy, had parted company. The authority of faith had been challenged and things were never to be the same again. Our story concerns that challenge as taken up by one man, John Wyclif of Oxford, and the far-reaching, often tragic, repercussions this was to have for many of the men and women who, during the 15th and 16th centuries, dwelt among the Chiltern Hills.

Early Heresy

It was a Briton called Pelagius who had given the Church one of its earliest heresies. He disagreed with one of the great Fathers of the Church, St Augustine of Hippo, over the concept of original sin and he questioned the concept of man's entire dependence on God for salvation. He preferred to think that man was captain of his own soul. Augustine himself, before he adopted orthodox Christianity, had dabbled in the very early Manichaean heresy which had spread to North Africa from 3rd century Persia, where it had flourished. During late Antiquity and the early Middle Ages, many of the heresies which emerged, for example, Montanism, Messalianism, Paulicianism and the Bogomil heresy, were to come almost entirely from the East, and Asia Minor.

In the 11th century, a Manichaean type of dualistic heresy came to light, this time in Western Europe, around Albi in the Languedoc area of southern France. The chronicler, Adhémar of Chabannes, tells of this, the Cathar heresy, and the strange behaviour of its adherents, the 'perfecti', who were soon to bring down upon themselves the wrath of the Albigensian Crusade and the newly formed Inquisition. The first burnings took place in Orleans in 1022. Western Europe was now to experience other heretical movements. In 1173, a rich young merchant of Lyons, called Valdes, taking literally the words of Jesus to the rich man, sold all his possessions and became a beggar. Another young man of similar background, John (nicknamed Francis) Bernadone of Assisi, was to do much the same thing. Both men attracted a following: but whereas St Francis did finally win papal approbation for his mendicant order, Valdes and his group did not. Nevertheless the sect grew. The Waldensians, as they were called, studied the Scriptures avidly and committed whole passages to memory. Persecuted and hounded from place to place throughout Europe, many were burnt. When the terrifying figure of Conrad of Marburg was let loose to seek out and destroy them, then for a time the process of the Inquisition took on the aspect of a massive witch hunt. For heresy and witchcraft were to become increasingly confused in the minds of even the most intelligent people. To try and win back wanderers from the faith, the new mendicant Orders of the Franciscans and Dominicans were sent into heretical territory. Devotion to the Rosary and to the Stations of the Cross was encouraged, pilgrimages were initiated and Third Orders founded in an effort to strengthen the orthodoxy. But all too often the persuasion of the sermon gave way to the harsher methods of the Inquisition.

Paradoxically, the Franciscans were themselves to produce an heretical group from among their number. These, the Fraticelli, were attracted back to the original ideals of St Francis and took the extreme measure of declaring their belief in the absolute poverty of Christ, thus threatening by implication the 'living standard' of the Church hierarchy, which could not be tolerated.

Medieval England and the Church

We can assume that from time to time in England, as in the rest of Europe, there were deviants: people who, theologically speaking, wanted, as we have seen, to go their own way; who criticised the Church and the illiteracy of many of its priests, together with the worldliness of its prelates. One has only to read Chaucer and Langland to sense an ongoing critical undercurrent. However, up till the end of the 14th century, there had been no great persecutions in England. The reason for this is that the machinery did not exist here: the Inquisition was never established in England. Furthermore, there was a basic difference between Roman and English Law. Whereas Roman Law was concerned with seeking the truth at any price, English Law was more concerned with keeping the King's peace, even if this meant compromise. A feature of Anglo-Saxon Law which lingered into the Middle Ages had demanded that wrongful or malicious accusers should themselves be punished, and this had deterred all but the most determined litigants. Even when requested by Pope Clement V to allow his inquisitors into England to proceed against the fabulously wealthy Order of Templars, Edward II had been reluctant to comply. Only the thought of getting his hands on some of the spoils had persuaded him to agree.

Of course England, with the rest of Western Christendom, was at that time subject to the magisterium of the Papacy, and therefore party to an ongoing conflict between Church and Monarchy – the Investiture Contest it is called – which flared up from time to time, between men like Charlemagne and Pope Leo III, between Emperor Henry IV and Pope Gregory VII, between Henry II of England and Archbishop Becket. Eventually Henry VIII of England sought to resolve forever this conflict in England by assuming for himself and his heirs the Supremacy of the Church here.

In medieval England there was a traditional resentment of papal interference in English Church affairs, of the appointment by the papacy of foreigners to English benefices and at papal taxation. So such measures as the Statutes of Praemunire and Provisors were introduced as an attempt to curb this interference. And, generally speaking, though by no means always, a guarded compromise existed between England and the Pope.

To this traditional reserve was added, as the 14th century progressed, a growing sense in England of national identity. England was no longer just an offshore French island: French was no longer the exclusive language at Court, where, increasingly, English was being introduced. Oxford scholars, like John Wyclif, were beginning to write in English rather than Latin. And more and more people were becoming literate. Lollardy responded to this vernacular literacy, spread and was persecuted because of it.

The Papacy

It is a remarkable fact that throughout the ages the Papacy has survived despite the vagaries of some of the individual holders of the office: and during the 14th century these vagaries reached a nadir. In 1309, because Rome was in a state of Imperial anarchy, Pope Clement V, a Frenchman, took up residence in Avignon. Strategically, Avignon was a good place to choose, and on the whole Avignon Popes were able men. But this was an unprecedented happening for the Church, and there were all kinds of fears, especially in England, of possible French influence on the Papacy. And then the Popes proceeded to build a magnificent palace and surrounded themselves with such opulence and administrative sophistication that, to all intents and purposes, they became temporal princes. Even before Avignon Aquinas had warned that 'the Pope has a plenitude of power like a king in a kingdom'. This manifestation of worldliness scandalised many of the clergy and laity, including scholars such as Dante Alighieri, Marsilius of Padua and the Franciscan William of Ockham, who universally called for Church reform. Marsilius felt that the Church should be subject to the State, while Ockham wanted it to be governed by councils. St Catherine of Siena simply compared the Papal court to a brothel. In 1378 two 'popes' were set up in rivalry with each other, and later a third contender claimed the title. In 1417 the schism was healed with the election of Oddo Colonna as Martin V, but by then the concept of the Papacy's seemingly unshakable plenitude of power had been severely damaged, and this was to play into Lollard hands.

The Black Death

During the 1340s and 50s, England, together with the rest of Europe, was to endure the horror of the Black Death. Medieval people were helpless before most catastrophes, and this one was to reduce the population by at least a third. Can one wonder at the fatalistic, almost magic-ridden attitude to life which crept in and filtered from the people to the Church, and perhaps back again? There emerged an attitude of almost bargaining with the Almighty against the Day of Judgement. But such horror could also evoke the idealism of the mystic, for Thomas à Kempis, Richard Rolle and Dame Julian of Norwich were also products of this time.

The devastation of the Black Death left in its wake all sorts of restlessness in England as well as Europe. A labourer was now worth more than his master, but his demand for higher wages created inflation. The depleted workforce now had room to try and negotiate for itself some small concessions in living standards, and the temptation to sell his labour to the highest bidder encouraged the labourer to move about in search of more generous wages. This was to spell doom to the old, ordered feudal society. And with the social bonds thus weakened, the whole concept of dominion or lordship was called into question. On this subject, Richard FitzRalph, Archbishop of Armagh, said:

> 'So far as I can judge, no man in a state of mortal sin has true lordship over other creatures in God's sight. He ought rather to be called a tyrant, a thief or a robber, though he may keep the name of a prince or lord by reason of hereditary succession, or the approval of the people subject to him, or by some human law. But

he has no true lordship until he repents, and until the grace of penance has restored him to a state acceptable to God.'

But the working man had his own, much simpler way of expressing his thoughts:

'When Adam delved and Eve span, who was then the gentleman?'

King and Court in 14th Century England

In medieval England it was vital that the King should be seen to rule. It is true that, as the centuries progressed, successive Kings tended to rule more 'in Council', but still it was they that ruled. If, for any reason, regency was necessary then it was important that this must not be allowed to go on too long.

The last years of Edward III's reign, in conjunction with the early years of Richard II's reign, form one of the most confused periods in English history. The situation was complicated by the renewal of the war with France and the need for money to pay for it. Particularly hard pressed were the lesser clergy - as poor as the hierarchy of the Church were rich – who now found themselves doubly taxed by Crown and Papacy.

The power vacuum which grew during Edward III's last ailing and failing years was contested on one hand by the Church party, and on the other by a party grouped around the princes of the blood, the Black Prince and his brother, John of Gaunt. The Church party was led by William of Wykeham, a very able administrator, who, during Edward's reign, had gained preferment from a nobody to a prince of the Church. As Bishop of Winchester and Chancellor of England, Wykeham possessed enormous power. The chronicler Froissart said of him, 'Everything passed through his hands. He stood so high in the King's favour that, in his time, everything was done in England by his consent, and nothing done without it'. At Court he was hated as an upstart, and Gaunt sought his downfall. In the 'Good Parliament' of 1376, Wykeham sided with the Commons in mistrusting Gaunt and demanding that Prince Richard, now that his father, the Black Prince, had died, should appear before them to be acknowledged as heir apparent. With justification, Wykeham and the Commons suspected Gaunt's motives: in February 1377, by Royal Charter, Gaunt's Dukedom of Lancaster was declared a Palatinate – a veritable 'imperium in imperio'. And, though at first this was granted only for Gaunt's lifetime, it later became an hereditary title. Onto this tense scene had come John Wyclif, for it was to him that Gaunt had turned in his vendetta against Wykeham. But here Wyclif was to incur the lasting opposition of William Courtenay, Bishop of London, who was Wykeham's supporter.

John Wyclif and his Supporters at Court

John was born about 1330 at Wyclif, near Richmond in Yorkshire. Since the Conquest, the Honour of Richmond had traditionally been associated with the counts and dukes of Brittany, but for a significant period of years, from 1342 to 1372, it passed to John of Gaunt, who thus became Wyclif's overlord. In about the year 1345 the young John Wyclif went up to Oxford, where he was to become the most brilliant scholar of his day. The University had admittedly been depleted of scholars by the ravages of the Black Death – William of Ockham, the most original philosopher of the Middle Ages, who had perished in the plague of 1349, had studied there – but Wyclif was brilliant by any standard, and rose through the Schools to become a Fellow of Merton and a Master of Balliol. Like many scholars of his day, Wyclif was outspoken in his attack on the institutional Church, and, for a time between 1371-8, Gaunt found a use for his fluent invective. In return Gaunt gave Wyclif protection, and no less a person than Joan of Kent, the Black Prince's wife, then widow, and soon to be Queen Mother, also befriended him. It has even been suggested that, had the Black Prince lived, he would have made a good Lollard! Perhaps, too, Wyclif was later to influence members of the retinue of Richard II's first wife, Anne of Bohemia. Certainly his teaching was to reach John Huss in that country and this may have been the route by which it travelled.

In addition to the royal family, there were certain knights at Court, men trusted by Joan of Kent, who were also to fall under Wyclif's spell – the 'hooded' knights they were called because of their lack of respect at refusing to bare their heads during Mass in the presence of the Host. They were a close-knit group of men: Sir Lewis Clifford, his son–in–law, Sir Philip de la Vache, Sir Thomas Latimer, Sir William Nevil, Sir John Clanvow, Sir John Montagu and Sir John Cheyne, to name some of them. Sir William Nevil's great-nephew, George, was a member of the Cheyne family of Beckford in Gloucester. These Cheynes were a cadet branch of the Cheynes of Drayton Beauchamp near Aston Clinton. They also possessed Grove Manor in Chesham and were later to acquire Chesham

Bois, Blackwell Hall Manor and Mordaunt's Fee. These were not landless knights but men of property and influence. The Cheynes were related by marriage to Sir John Clanvow and Sir John Oldcastle. The latter was to become a veritable Lollard firebrand and was to lead later members of the family into all kinds of trouble. For it has to be said that their aesthetic motive in adhering to Wyclif's doctrine was tinged with a certain greed for power. They saw, as Gaunt had seen, the possibility of getting their hands on Church property, and this was to lead them to dabble in treason. But by then heresy and treason had become inextricably bound together.

Wyclif's Teaching and his Disciples at Oxford and Leicester

It is important to understand that Wyclif's descent into heresy was progressive and embodied in a mass of tortuous literature. At first there was nothing startling in his doctrine of dominion by grace, of his veneration of the Bible and his claim for its infallibility, of his distinction between the earthly, or institutional, church and the heavenly church, or his theory of foreknown, irreversible election. Augustine, FitzRalph and Bradwardine had said much the same thing. But Wyclif went on positively to dismiss the institutional church out of hand, and this was his heresy. From here it was a logical progression for him to doubt the need for clergy and to question their sacramental efficacy, even to question the sacramental mystery of the Mass itself.

On Sunday, 21st June 1377, old King Edward died, to be succeeded by the child King Richard, so that one weak situation gave way to another, in which Gaunt was to remain all-powerful. But powerful as he was, Gaunt was finding Wyclif's hardening theological deviation difficult to 'live with'. In February of that year, in his efforts to protect his protégé from Courtenay's attacks, Gaunt and his ally Henry Percy, Earl of Northumberland and Marshal of England, had fallen foul of the London mob, an independent bred, who hated them both and proved a match even for the great Percy. So Gaunt took the safest course and gradually dropped Wyclif from his service, though both he and Joan of Kent continued to give Wyclif protection. Wyclif made his last political appearance in October, 1378.

Oxford had been Wyclif's first sphere of influence and it was there, probably to the Queen's College, that he was to return for just a few more years. And once more he was to gather round himself a group of disciples, John Aston, Laurence Steven, Robert Alington, John Ashwardby; and two who were very important for Chesham, Nicholas Hereford and Philip Repingdon. Hereford, a doctor of divinity and an early admirer of Wyclif, was engaged on an English translation of the Bible, while Repingdon, a more recent convert, was studying for his doctorate. These two men were Austin canons from the great Abbey of St Mary in the Meadows at Leicester.

In those days before 1381, so heady and careless for the young Lollards, Philip and Nicholas were able to move freely from Oxford to Leicester, and where they influenced a 'parchemyner', William Smith – parchmenters and scriveners were, for obvious reasons in the vanguard of the Lollard movement – who began copying out Wyclif's treatises. Smith formed a conventicle in a deserted chapel in Leicester, where he was joined by Swinderby or 'William the Hermit', as he was known. Swinderby was an unbeneficed mass priest who had already gone on several preaching tours, spreading his own brand of puritanical teaching, and using as a headquarters a cell in the very Abbey itself. He was a member of the clerical underworld through which a new, popularised, less academic form of Wyclif's teaching was ultimately to travel the length and breadth of England and into the very Marches of Wales. And, paradoxically, it must be questioned whether Wyclif the scholar would have wanted things to go the way they did: whether he would have approved of the direct, almost crude language and argument of some of the later Lollards. But he was not to have his say in how the movement was to develop. For he was only to inspire it, not to lead it.

Leicester Abbey and Its Canons: The Chesham Connection

Soon Leicester was rife with the new teaching, the only other known centre of it outside Oxford in those early days. But before long, nearby daughter cells were being set up at Melton Mowbray, Hallaton, Market Harborough and Loughborough, thanks to Swinderby's travelling sermons. Why were those early Leicester days so carefree? Well, we have seen the unsettled state of England and the depths to which the Papacy had sunk. Both the nation and the Church were too preoccupied to bother too much about this group of young hotheads. Archbishop Sudbury should have seen what was happening, but he did nothing. Nearer home, Bishop Buckingham of Lincoln was very slow to act, and when he did eventually move against Swinderby, he was content merely to push him out of his jurisdiction and leave it at that. The Abbot of Leicester, William Kereby, elected in 1377, seems to have been very easy-going and ignorant of what was happening under his very nose: it has been suggested that he may even have been sympathetic to the Lollard cause! John of Gaunt, Earl of Leicester, who in any case had been in the habit of befriending Swinderby in the past, now took the entire situation under his protection. In other words, all the conditions were right for the plant to take firm root.

The canons Hereford and Repingdon also went on preaching trips to outlying parishes from time to time. On one occasion, Hereford is known to have travelled as far as Odiham in Hampshire, and so effective was his eloquence that an important centre of Lollardy was to grow here. We know also that Repingdon preached an heretical sermon at Brackley in Northamptonshire. It was, of course, quite usual for Austin canons to act as visiting preachers, especially if, as with Brackley, they owned the patronage: and they very often provided vicars for their own churches from members of their House. This was all part of the tradition of their Order. Now Leicester Abbey possessed the patronage of a great many churches, and it would have been impossible for canons of that House to have manned every one of them or visited them regularly to preach. But, even so, it is accepted that they did endeavour to live up to the traditions of their Order in this respect.

One of the churches in the possession of Leicester Abbey was none other than the church of Chesham. It had been given to them by the Sifrewast family back in the 12th century, and they shared its patronage with the Cistercian Abbey at Woburn. So, in other words, at the very inception of the Lollard movement, its first known apostles were Chesham's rectors, with preaching rights in the church, which they may well have exercised, together with the right to present vicars here. And if they required hospitality near Chesham, then they needed to look no further than Missenden Abbey, also an Austin House. There were close ties between the two Abbeys, for William Bradele of Leicester Abbey had become Abbot of Missenden in 1348.

Once outside Gaunt's sphere of influence, where else could the canons look for protection? Where else but to that group of hooded knights we have already met, some of whom possessed property and influence nearby? When, much later, Hereford was 'on the run' he could count on one of them, Montagu of Shenley in Hertfordshire, to shelter him: while Nevil, another of them, was to try desperately to save him from the wrath of Archbishop Courtenay, even to the extent of offering to stand bail for him. It is also known that these knights had guards mounted in their own churches in order to protect Lollard preachers. It has, in fact, recently been put forward that, during the first thirty years of its life, the Lollard movement was given sufficient protection by this group of devoutly heretical courtiers to ensure that strongholds, like that in the Chilterns, could take irreversible root. Their adherence to Lollardy was to remain constant during this period, even after the demise or recantation of the original academic bloc.

Did Repingdon or Hertford visit Chesham on their journeys between Oxford and Leicester, or on official Abbey business, or later when they were in hiding? Did the people of Chesham hear from their lips a very early, pure and uncorrupted brand of Lollard teaching? To this the answer must be perhaps, possibly more, but certainly no less!

1382: A Year of Decision

1382 was to be the year of decision for the infant scholastic Lollard movement. In 1381 the Peasants' Revolt had erupted in England as a result of fresh efforts to raise money for the French Wars. A new tax, the Poll Tax, had been brought in and there had been two attempts to collect it, in 1377 and again in 1379. This, coupled with the corruption of the tax collectors, brought matters to a head. It was from the Home Counties, from Essex, Kent and the Thames Valley, that the rebels, led by Wat Tyler and John Ball, drew their strength. At the height of the rebellion, Archbishop Sudbury was slain, and there occurred the famous confrontation between the rebels and the boy King Richard. The rebels were profoundly loyal to the person of the King: their watchword was, 'With whom hold you?' the answer being, 'With King Richard and the true commons'. The ringleaders demanded the abolition of the Statute of Labourers, the Poll Tax and the commutation of service to rent payment. The young King made promises and the peasants dispersed, but not before Tyler had also lost his life.

The Peasants' Revolt was bound to compromise the Lollard cause. Inevitably the chroniclers Walsingham and Knighton (another canon of Leicester Abbey, as it happens) blamed Wyclif for inciting the ringleaders. Knighton likened John Ball to Wyclif's 'John the Baptist'. The name 'Lollard', not a particularly new word, had previously meant 'mumbler', 'idle fellow': but after the Revolt, with Lollardy emerging as a scapegoat for every kind of disturbance, 'Lollard' now came to mean the medieval equivalent of anything from 'red' to 'fascist pig'. In vain did Wyclif deny any complicity in the rising. He actually found the whole episode obnoxious, but it was useless to protest. And in all honesty it took but little imagination to interpret his attack on dominion as 'slander to make discourse and dissention between the various estates both temporal and spiritual to the commotion of the people and the great peril of the whole realm'.

In spring, 1382, the redoubtable Courtenay succeeded the murdered Sudbury as Archbishop of Canterbury. For him the mixture of sedition and heresy had gone quite far enough. After the 'Earthquake Council', held at Blackfriars in London, he wasted no time in going straight for the Oxford ringleaders. They, in their turn, staged one last desperate fling, preaching inflammatory sermons and hurling defiance at the Archbishop. But these scholars were ultimately not made of the stuff of martyrs: they were men with a social conscience rather than fanatics, and they crumbled before Courtenay's direct onslaught.

So Courtenay was successful in crushing the academic side of the Lollard movement. But it was not till 1389 that he got round to visiting Leicester Abbey to deal with William Smith, and he could be accused of 'shutting the stable door after the horse has gone', for, as we have seen, he was several moves behind the spreading doctrine. The word had reached folk who could be capable of martyrdom, and there was no stopping it now.

And what of Wyclif during this time? He had finally retired to his rectory at Lutterworth, given to him by Gaunt, where he was left in peace by Courtenay, and where, assisted by his amanuensis, John Purvey, he spent his last days probably translating into English his beloved Bible. He died in 1384.

Of our two Austin canons, Hereford held out longest, until 1391, spending most of the intervening time, apart from a trip to Rome, in the West Country, where he taught Lollard beliefs. Swinderby and Purvey were also to flee there, and Bristol became a Lollard centre, whence later teachers were to come into the Chilterns, as we shall see. When Nicholas finally recanted, he was given the chancellorship of Hereford Cathedral as a reward.

Repingdon 'cracked' quite spectacularly in the autumn of 1382 and, for his ostensible return to orthodoxy, was in due course also suitably preferred. In 1393 he replaced Abbot Kereby as Abbot of Leicester, and there he remained as Chesham's patron, until 1404. There followed several terms of office as Chancellor of Oxford University and then, having already become confessor and confidant to the new King Henry IV, in 1405 he replaced Henry Beaufort as Bishop of Lincoln. How well did Repingdon perform the office of Bishop? Lincoln was an enormous diocese, but it is agreed that Repingdon was very conscientious, even to the extent of interfering in the affairs of his old Abbey at Leicester. It used to be claimed that he was a zealous persecutor of Lollards, and a glance at his Register does seem to give that impression. He appears to throw up his hands in horror at the prevalence of heresy 'longe et late per nostras civitatem et diocesim'. A closer look, however, reveals a great deal of talk, but very little action. Plans are constantly put forward for the suppression of heresy, but nothing ever happens. A more recent assessment of Repingdon claims that, although outwardly orthodox, he never gave up his old Lollard sentiments, even to the extent of remaining on friendly terms with notorious Lollards. Did this influence, as Abbot of our patronal House and as our Bishop, leave its mark on Chesham? The list of Chesham Leicester's vicars contains one or two suspect names which might repay further investigation. John Woodard, instituted in 1404, bears the same name as a Lollard chaplin who had been active under Latimer's patronage, in Northamptonshire. Richard Monk, a notorious heretic, who originated from Melton Mowbray where Swinderby had been active and who appears in Archbishop Chichele's Register, was appointed vicar here in Chesham in 1421, just as Bishop Repingdon's term of office was drawing to its close. Two other suspicious names must be mentioned here, even though no direct connection with Repingdon can possibly be claimed at this stage. Thomas Bolle was vicar of Chesham Leicester some time after 1434, but only his resignation is recorded, so we have no idea of his previous parish. But we do know that a Thomas Bolle had, between 1402 and 1430, been vicar at Brackley, one of Leicester Abbey's churches where Repingdon preached all those years ago. Of John Gamelyngay we have only the evidence of the will of John Wynslowe, citizen and draper of London, who had leased the manor of Chesham Bois. One of the executors of the will, dated 12th July, 1423, which leaves four shillings to the fabric of Chesham Church, was John Gamelyngay, 'vicar of Chesham'. It may be mere coincidence that the Patent and Close Rolls for 1395 record how a Fellow of Merton, John Gamelyngay, was imprisoned in Beaumaris Castle, along with other heretics. But, again, it would be worth investigating.

A New King and Sedition

King Richard's reign had never been an easy one, dominated as it was by his struggle against his would-be masters and the Appellant Lords. Of late, he had come increasingly to rely on the stabilising influence of his uncle, Gaunt, who, in spite of having incurred earlier suspicion, had nevertheless demonstrated his undying loyalty to his nephew, a loyalty which remained unshaken even when Richard foolishly banished Gaunt's son Henry Bolingbroke. On 3rd February 1399, old Gaunt died and Richard committed the ultimate folly of confiscating his banished cousin's vast Lancaster inheritance. Bolingbroke invaded England to claim his Palatinate and, in October of that year, he snatched the Crown of England too.

It followed that the new King viewed all subversion as a threat to his shaky throne. And, if, once upon a time, Chaucer had seen fit to treat Lollards as something of a joke, to be so accused now was no longer a laughing matter. For, in 1401 was passed the Statute for the burning of Heretics, which spelt out the people it was intended to deal with:

'They make unlawful conventicles and confederacies,
   they hold and exercise schools, they make and write
   books, they do wickedly instruct and inform people'.

The Lollards, no less!

But even now, the English Church was reluctant to go to such extremes of extermination, and, like Repingdon, preferred to turn a blind eye to heresy, if they could get away with it. There may even have been some sympathy for the highest ideals of Lollardy provided these were privately and sincerely professed, and by people of noble or at least gentle birth. Repingdon had been and was to remain a close and influential friend of King Henry IV. So toleration was to remain the norm, especially where offenders could boast of aristocratic patronage: and only twice, between 1401 and 1413, was the extreme penalty invoked against the Lollards.

1414 was to be another decisive year for the Lollard movement. Henry IV had died on March 20th 1413, and his son, Hal, the erstwhile playboy prince, was very soon to demonstrate just how seriously he now took himself as King of England. In the very next year he was faced with a rebellion, now led by his old comrade, Sir John Oldcastle, who, as a boy in

The sentencing and absolution of Thomas Harding.
(*Woodcut from: John Foxe, Acts & Monuments (1570)*

His relapse after abjuration made him liable to the writ of 'de heretico comburendo' and death.

The martyrdom of Tyndale, 1536. *(John Foxe: The Book of Martyrs. 1563. This was a lavishly produced book illustrated by many woodcuts and was the largest project undertaken in Britain at that time.)*

Herefordshire, had learnt his Lollard beliefs from none other than Swinderby.

The abortive rebellion which Oldcastle led to St Giles's Field was heavily supported by men from the Chilterns, brought there by the Cheynes, Roger and his sons, Thomas and John. As has already been suggested, Chesham may perhaps have been initiated into the Lollard heresy much earlier, but it is generally accepted that, around 1414, the Cheynes of Drayton Beauchamp were the most important Lollard influence in the Chilterns. (They were to introduce a notorious Lollard, Thomas Drayton, into their living at Drayton Beauchamp, who in his turn, is said to have influenced John Angret, parson of Latimer.) Precisely when and from whom they had picked up their heresy we do not know. The Beckford Cheynes or Oldcastle himself may have been responsible for introducing them to it. But however they had come by it, it is obvious that they had had time to nurture a cohesive group of Chesham Lollards, in time to lead them to St Giles's Field.

This rebellion was to show how far Lollardy had become compromised with treason. Oldcastle always claimed that Richard II was still alive, and it was his intention to overthrow the new King and seize power himself. William Morley, a brewer of Dunstable, carried a pair of spurs with him to the rebellion, in anticipation of a knighthood after Oldcastle's victory.

Young King Henry had been tipped off about the planned uprising. He just waited for the isolated and disorganised bands of rebels to straggle into London before springing the trap: and, unlike his father, he was to have no scruples about burning the culprits. After all, he had witnessed the burning of Badby, the Lollard, back in 1409, with no signs of squeamishness.

Of the Chiltern Group, John Horwood and John Winchester, both Amersham men, suffered the ultimate penalty. Roger Cheyne was to die before his release from the Tower. John Cheyne was pardoned after a few months, but his brother, Thomas, the most active Cheyne Lollard, had to wait longer, until 1415, for release along with other lesser men, such as Thomas Sibley, Robert Sprotford, John Langacre and Robert Norton, and many more who had chanced fame and fortune at St Giles's Field.

For a long time, Oldcastle managed to avoid capture, using the now well-organised underground Lollard network which had grown up over the years. To his would-be captors, Oldcastle was everywhere and nowhere. But, finally, in 1419, he was taken and dealt with.

In 1431 another uprising was to take place, led by William Perkins, and it is possible the Cheynes sent some support to it, for John was arrested and he and his brother were summoned before the Council, while their Library was searched for books. But there is no firm evidence that they were implicated, and this rising was not of the same scale and magnitude as St Giles had been.

How the Lollards Survived

The Lollards had, as we have seen, lost their academic evangelists as long ago as 1382. The new movement had been protected through the next thirty years by men like the Cheynes: but now, in 1431, all vestiges of aristocratic patronage were to vanish. Henceforth Lollardy was to be a cult of the lower orders only, of artisans and craftsmen such as weavers and cordwainers and glovers (and there were many such in Chesham!). There was no common organisation to unite them; they survived in subversive groups which reached from Kent and East Anglia, through London and the Chilterns and Berkshire, Wiltshire and Bristol and the Marches of Wales, and up to the Midlands. Secrecy and flexibility were their watchwords. Danger was not openly courted, heroism was not sought, and many recanted before the threat of the stake. But in the last extremity many Lollards could and did prove to be very brave. Within these groups of devout men and women family tradition was often strong – the Scriveners of Amersham and the Mordens of Chesham illustrate this. And, although they had to all intents and purposes formed an alternative 'church', in a large number of cases they were outwardly conforming to the established church. The great amount of 15th century church building and enlarging (and St Mary's Church in Chesham can bear witness) even in Lollard country, is evidence of this conformity, as is the will of Marian Morden of Chesham, which is a model of orthodoxy.

And what were the beliefs which they held so dear that they were often prepared to die for them? Some of the doctrines of these later Lollards contain some very strident, revolutionary ideas. They were against the Pope, who, for them was Antichrist; they were against clerical possessions, the need for baptism, or need for formal marriage ceremonies: they were against the existence of purgatory, the veneration of saints or their images or the need for pilgrimages: they were against the need for confession to a priest especially if he himself was in a state of mortal sin, the need for bells, organs and singing in church: and, of course, they were against the doctrine of transubstantiation. All of this, you could say, was their negative doctrine. But, positively, they were for the Bible, and its translation into English. They were 'Bible men', the 'just fast men', the 'known men'. The Bible and its study were central to their faith. Those who could read, read aloud to those who could not. There was the impetus to learn for themselves and possess the Scriptures. They would even learn whole passages off by heart – as the Waldensians had done. There was a flourishing underground market for books, and, before the introduction of printing, scriveners were vital to this market. There was no sex discrimination among readers and expounders of the Scriptures. If a woman showed talent in this direction, then she was listened to. Lollards were especially fond of St Luke's Gospel, together with St Paul's Epistles and the Epistle of St James, which they frequently knew by heart.

The Later Lollards of the Chilterns

The last half of the 15th century was more or less taken up in England with the murderous rivalry between Lancaster and York, which was seen by some later Lollards as judgement upon a corrupt nation. There were to be several minor episodes of Lollard persecution in the Chilterns area during the 1440s and 50s, when we hear of the prosecution of Thomas Bickenore of Wallingford, Richard Preston of Cookham and John Gutter, a wanderer of no fixed address. But a major persecution was to be initiated in 1462, by Bishop Chedworth, who had come to the See of Lincoln in 1452. And, if previously Lollards had for the most part been anonymous believers, from now on names came tumbling out of the Bishop's Registers, to be canonised later by the 16th century martyrologist, Foxe. At this time, too, we begin to see how the Lollard movement was being 'worked back' from the West Country to the Chilterns in the person of James Willis, called sometimes the apostle of the Chiltern Hills. Born in Bristol about 1403, a weaver by trade, Willis was literate and could remember being taught his heresy by William, a Smith by name and trade (but not the Leicester Smith). Willis left Bristol about 1450 to become a wandering preacher and found his way to London, where he was imprisoned, and where he was eventually returned for execution. He seems, after his release, to have got to the Thames Valley, to Henley, Marlow and Hambledon and also to Princes Risborough, Wycombe, Amersham and Chesham: and he put new heart into the Chiltern Lollards. His disciples included John Polley of Henley, and at Amersham he taught John Conwyrk, Thomas Scrivener, and Geffrey Simeon. John Baron, John

Crane and Richard Body, all of Amersham, come to light now. There were other Amersham teachers at this time, a man called Pope and another called Patrick. At Chesham the outstanding teacher then was John White, but some of those brought to trial claimed that they had been taught by the rector of Chesham Bois. Was this a case of mistaken identity with Richard Monk of Chesham? In any case, the practice among some suspected Lollards, who were required to name others of their kind, was to name people already dead.

Many of those accused of heresy during this persecution of Bishop Chedworth were forced to perform a ritual of penance at Wycombe first, where the scene was witnessed by Chedworth himself in company with the Bishop of Exeter; then there was a second performance at Aylesbury, and lastly at Thame. One man, who escaped death in 1464, John Goose by name, was to suffer death at the stake ten years later at Tower Hill. He met his end with great courage, having first been given a good supper by Robert Billesdon, Sheriff of London.

The next important persecution took place in 1511, when 'a godly and great company' of people were found to be heretics by Bishop Smith. It is here that we first hear of Thomas Harding, so my part of the story is nearly done. Let it suffice to say that this particular persecution centred on Amersham, which had become the Chiltern headquarters of the Lollard heresy, in fact the town was virtually controlled by them. William Tylesworth, William Scrivener, Robert Cosin and Nicholas Colyns lost their lives at the stake and Thomas Chase died of his injuries received while a prisoner of the Bishop: many others were branded on the cheek or made to wear the heretics' badge of the crossed faggot. It was from Amersham that Thomas Harding was to come and settle in Chesham.

It would I think be fitting for me to end with a true Chesham Lollard, one of whom Wyclif himself would have been proud, one who embodied all that was central to the Lollard creed. In the year 1521, Bishop Longland of Lincoln embarked on a fresh persecution of Lollards, which was to bring to light John Morden of Chesham, from whom his son-in-law, Richard Ashford, had learnt his heresy. In teaching Ashford, Morden had said:

'Thou art deceived for it can nothing profitt thee, for it is but bred and wyne, and so it is when the priest begane with it at masse and so it is when the masse is ended. Also the images be but stocks and stones, for they cannot help themself, how can they help thee? And worshipping of them is but idolatrie. And there is no pilgrimage here in this world but one brother go with another in the unity and the Law of God after such knowledge as I have'.

Lollardy and the Reformation: Postscript

On 12th May, 1521, Cardinal Wolsey presided over the burning of Luther's books in St Paul's Churchyard, so from now on we can no longer think of Lollardy in isolation. The new German ideas were being heard in England. Had the Lollards done anything to help or hinder the Reformation? In one way they had prepared the ground for a very deep-rooted religious revolution, but on the other hand they had sufficiently awakened the authorities to the existence of heresy for the machinery of persecution to be ready to deal with it. There could be no Reformation without royal consent. Henry VIII only broke with Rome for his own ends, but he was still defender of the seven sacraments and had no sympathy with heresy. England had to wait till the next reign to become a truly Protestant country and was finally to settle officially for the compromise of Anglicanism. Meanwhile, what of the Lollards? Theologically, we can look for them with the Quakers, and as such they were to suffer yet more persecution. Politically, well, why not ask Roger Crab? For Lollards and Levellers had much in common.

PART 2: The Life and Death of Thomas Harding

The Earlier Proceedings against Thomas Harding

The capital charge against Thomas Harding in 1532 was one of relapse into heresy, because he had already formally abjured all heresy before Bishop William Smyth, who died in 1514. Relapse after abjuration made him liable to the writ of 'de heretico comburendo' under the statute of 1401. Even Joan of Arc submitted to such formal abjuration; it was this that enabled the English to burn a saint.

The original proceedings against Thomas Harding were connected with the burning of William Tylesworth at Amersham, said by Foxe to have taken place in 1506, though this seems to be some years too early. Among the sixty Lollards who had to bear faggots on this occasion were five

Hardings, including Thomas and Alice his wife. The penance imposed on them both under pain of relapse was to 'wear a signe of a fagot of diverse colours upon ther uttermost garment durying their lyffes' and to 'fast brede and ale every Corpus Christi evyn'. This was less severe than fasting on bread and water.

On 24th April 1515, at Missenden Abbey, this penance was relaxed, at least as far as the faggot badges were concerned, by Bishop William Atwater; but Thomas and Alice were not to dwell out of Amersham, and were to go on Corpus Christi day in the procession at the College of the Precious Blood at Ashridge, barefoot and bare-legged, bearing a taper of wax, in such place as should be assigned to them by the prior or sub-rector there.

It seems clear that the Hardings willingly accepted this annual pilgrimage to Ashridge, which had an alleged relic of the Precious Blood of Christ, to which a contemporary poet refers:

> 'The Bonhommes of Ashridge beside Berkhamsted,
> That goodly place, to Skelton most kind,
> Where the sang royal is, Christ's blood so red,
> A pleasanter place than Ashridge is, hard were to find.'

At Ashridge there was a clear distinction between the natural or physical blood of Christ, some part of which could still exist on earth, and the presence of His Body and Blood in the Eucharist, in which His sacrificed humanity is imparted to us under the forms of bread and wine. Without compromising his belief that the natural body of Christ was not now on earth, Harding could venerate the blood which was shed for us in the Passion, that blood-shedding which, as he said, was his salvation. The relic was destroyed in 1539 when the College was dissolved and Ashridge became the nursery and playground of the future King Edward VI.

On 22nd April 1518 Thomas Harding appeared before Bishop Atwater at his court of audience in the chapter-house at Ashridge to settle a dispute involving him and Robert Baldwyn of the parish of Aston Clinton (actually of St Leonard's, which was then in that parish) concerning a chaplaincy at Little Missenden parish church which, according to Thurstan Martyn's representative, they were to maintain for a year for Thurstan's soul. Baldwyn was ordered (and promised) to maintain the chaplain at his own expense for six months, but no order was made against Harding, and nothing more is heard of the matter. It may be relevant that three years later the Vicar of Little Missenden and nine of his parishioners were accused of Lollardy.

Bishop Atwater was succeeded by 1521 by John Longland, a zealous persecutor of Lollards. Thomas Harding was implicated in several confessions made before him at Amersham, and was himself examined under oath, but made no statement that incriminated himself or anyone else. Longland found him guilty not of heresy but of perjury in failing to detect others, and sentenced him to wear a patch of green cloth, embroidered like a faggot, before and behind.

Thomas Harding moves to Chesham

By 1522 Harding had moved to 'Chessam Waterside', where he had a smallholding. The Muster Certificates of that year show that he had goods to the value of £32, which put him into the top ten in the parish of Great Chesham. At Great Missenden he had land but no goods. There was another Thomas Harding in Chesham, who lived in the Town (Waterside being one of the eight hamlets) and had goods worth £13.6s.8d. In the Subsidy Roll of 1524 this Thomas Harding is distinguished as a mercer; he was then taxed on £10, and our Thomas on £20. There were only five higher assessments than this in Great Chesham, but apparently the larger landowners paid their tax elsewhere.

The association of Thomas Harding with Dungrove Farm, mentioned on his memorial, rests on tradition, supported by the name Harding's Walk for a footpath from the farmhouse to Springfield Road; but there was another Thomas Harding of Botley who died in the same year, leaving a son Thomas. At the time of his conviction, our Thomas held a messuage in Chesham and four acres of copyhold, also in the manor of Chesham Higham. The former may well have been in the Town; the latter probably in Dungrove Field, which at this period was still divided, at least in part, into open-field strips, some of which were held by people of the Town, as the early deeds of Broadway Baptist Church show. There was no formal Enclosure in Chesham; the strips disappeared by gradual consolidation. Clearly Harding belonged to the rising class of farmers, about which his wife Alice had some doubts. She had said of Richard Bartlet of Amersham 'Here cometh a good man and I hope he will be a good man; but he hath so much mind of buying and selling and taking of farms that it putteth his mind from all goodness'. His brother Robert Bartlet told Alice that 'he had thought to have called William Tylsworth false heretic, but now he was better advised'. Mistress Harding said, 'I am glad you are converted to grace, and chosen to Almighty God. Never forsake that you are called to; for if you do, there is no hope for you'. This sounds like proto-Calvinist language, but St Augustine's doctrines of election and final perseverance were widely held and were not specifically Lollard. Isabel Treacher, who would not go to church on the numerous holy days, put her daughter in service with Alice Harding 'because she could instruct her better than many others'. Statements were made during the Bishop's enquiry at Amersham that many 'known men' (the local term for Lollards) resorted to the Harding's house, and when they disapproved of prayers at the church they did not join in; but all this fell short of proving heresy against them, and the Amersham 'conventicle' or house-church met elsewhere. The Bishop did not object to their moving to Chesham, where dissidents were fewer than at Amersham.

Nothing is known of Thomas Harding's life in Chesham between 1524 and 1532 except what can be gathered from the manor court rolls, from his own laconic statements at the Old Temple and from Foxe's narrative, which was obtained from informants in Amersham, not in Chesham. The usual feelings of the former town towards the latter may have slightly coloured Foxe's account of the 'rude rabble' of officers of the town who 'like mad men, ran desperately to his house in search for books, and searching went so nigh that under the boards of his floor they found certain English books of Holy Scripture'.

Thomas Harding's Books

Until 1526 at earliest, and probably for some years more, the books of Scripture kept and read by Thomas Harding must have been Wyclifite manuscripts, but the New Testament in English, which he had within one year before his arrest, was almost certainly Tyndale's translation. There are several ways in which he could have obtained it. In 1530 a company of Lollards met in the house of John Taylor of Hughenden to hear Nicholas Field from London, who had been in 'Almany' (Germany and the Low Countries). Among those present was William Hawks of Chesham. Another possible link could have been through John Ryburn of Risborough, who had met a priest called Thomas Lound who had spent two years in Wittenburg. It is significant that Ryburn said 'The blood of our Lord Jesus Christ hath made satisfaction for all ill deeds that are done or shall be done ...... If we ask pardon of our Lord Jesus Christ, He will give us pardon every day'. These were Thomas Harding's beliefs.

By whatever means, Harding had obtained other English books printed on the Continent. The 'Obedience of a Christian Man', which he was reading at the Martyr's Stile going into Hodd's Wood at the time of his arrest, was not 'a book of English prayers' as Foxe claimed, but a polemical tract by Tyndale. The 'Sum of Scripture in English' was probably a translation of a Latin treatise by Henricus Bomelius (Hendrick van Bommel) which was among the first to disseminate the Reformers' teaching on justification by faith. The British Museum Library copy has its title page damaged, so that its date is uncertain; the Library's guess is c.1535, but it seems that it was available a few years earlier. Justification by faith was not a distinctively Lollard doctrine, because of their emphasis on men's working out their salvation through holy living, but equally it was not a heresy; Luther's teaching on this point was widely accepted, and is compatible with that of the Council of Trent.

As regards the books of Scripture, Bishop Longland is said to have declared in 1521 that whoever read the Bible in English was damned, but when Harding was brought before him with his books on 6th April 1532 the Bishop knew only too well that King Henry VIII, at the outset of More's ministry, had already decided to have a translation 'in his hands ready to be given to his people, as he might see their manners and behaviour meet, apt and convenient to receive the same'. In fact Coverdale's version, published in 1535, was substantially Tyndale's; it is still in use in the Prayer Book Psalter, and a good deal of the wording still survives intact in the Revised Standard Version, which has ecumenical approval. In any event translation into the vernacular had a long history in England. The Venerable Bede had died while translating St John's Gospel into Old Northumbrian. Aelfric had translated much of the Bible into late West Saxon. The Wyclifite translation into Middle English had been widely read in the 15th century, and Henry VI, whose canonisation was considered imminent, had given a copy to the Charterhouse.

Thomas Harding and the King's Marriage

Probably the book which placed Harding in immediate and deadly peril was Tyndale's tract 'The Practice of Prelates' which condemned the equivocation of the English bishops in the matter of the King's marriage.

Harding was only too literally playing with fire. If, as seems certain, he approved of what he was reading, he must have condemned the King's brutal treatment of Queen Katherine of Aragon, who at the time was living in retirement at Ampthill, and was held in special regard in Buckinghamshire and Bedfordshire for her charity, particularly as a patron of lace-making; she is said to have been the inventor of Kat Stitch, which takes eight bobbins to a pin instead of four like other stitches.

The King's case was that the rule against marrying one's brother's widow was a divine law which no Pope or human legislator could dispense. The King's closest advisor, Sir Thomas More, the Lord Chancellor, then on the point of resignation, was in agreement with Tyndale, and with nearly all the theologians who were not bribed or threatened by Henry and his allies, that the rule was only a matter of ecclesiastical discipline. In particular, the Continental Protestants were dead against the King. There was indeed a prior question which was too dangerous to pursue: had Katherine's marriage to Henry's brother been consummated? If not, the King was a cad and a cheat. Bishop Longland had been the King's confessor and almost certainly knew the facts. He could not of course make any use of such knowledge, and in any case he had already decided to accept the King's claim to be Supreme Head of the Church, and to go all lengths with him. Longland decided not to proceed any further in the matters raised by the prohibited books; he adjourned the hearing until the 8th April and then examined Harding on other subjects.

Thomas Harding before the Bishop of Lincoln

The procedure in the Bishop's court was inquisitorial; Harding was under oath to reply to questions concerning the health of his soul. In the King's courts he would have been permitted (indeed required) to remain silent; the prosecution would have had to formulate precise charges against him, and then bring evidence to prove them beyond reasonable doubt. The right to silence is the glory of the English criminal procedure, and an essential feature of its accusatorial character. It was an anomalous and disgraceful feature of the Act of 1401 that it allowed what was in effect a death sentence to be imposed by a court in which the accused could be required to incriminate himself. In 1534 the ex-officio jurisdiction of the Bishops in cases of heresy was transferred to the Crown (which thereby acquired the offenders' estates), so that if Harding had lived two years longer he might at least have had a fair trial for his life, though his estate would have been in jeopardy. In 1535 Sir Thomas More relied on silence, and it took perjured evidence to secure a conviction. A later Act which made silence treasonable was generally regarded as an infamous blot on the statute book.

The second day of the examination was concerned with purgatory and with veneration of saints and images. Harding stated, quite accurately, that he could not find purgatory in the Scripture, but he found heaven and hell. The belief in intermediate states between death and the Last Judgement is certainly Scriptural, and their nature is clearly different for different souls, but Scripture is silent on whether one of these is a state of penal cleansing. Many of the Fathers of the Church had taught that hell itself involves such cleansing. Less than a century before, the Council of Florence had left it an open question whether purgatory is a place distinct from heaven and hell. In medieval England visual or dramatic representations of the 'Harrowing of Hell' were frequent, and conveyed the message that rebellious souls could still hear the gospel and live. However, the ordinary teaching of the Roman Church in the late Middle Ages was that purgatory was a distinct place, where the temporal punishment due to our forgiven sins is exacted; but that the Church has power to draw upon the 'treasury of merits' of Christ and the saints, and thus to extend indulgences, that is, remissions of such penalties, even into the unseen world. This claim had a great effect on the belief and practice of the more affluent classes; Henry VII had made provision for thirty thousand masses for his soul, and chantry foundations were multiplying, often under the control of lay trustees, as at Little Missenden; but it is questionable whether the religion of the common people was equally affected. One can read scores of English medieval religious poems on the two ways, to heaven and to hell, without finding any allusion to the intermediate state.

The exchanges with Harding on the adoration of the saints seem to have turned on the ambiguity in the Latin adoratio or the English worship. It is of course basic Christian doctrine that God wholly and alone is to be worshipped and revered with adoration; but in Middle or Early Modern English 'worship' could be applied to one's wife or to the Mayor, or in classical Latin (by 1532 everyone was trying to write classically) 'adoratio' could be used for the salutation, honour or reverence paid to saints or angels, or even to holy objects such as the cross, the Gospel book or icons. The Bishop was not an idolater, and he should have accepted Harding's statement that 'no saints are to be adored unless as great as

God', which is of course true if adoration is taken as the true worship of faith, which belongs to God alone.

Thomas Harding and the Passion

It was during this session that Thomas Harding insisted that Christ shed His blood for him, that this blood-shedding was his salvation and that the Passion of Christ was imprinted on his heart. Devotion to the humanity of Christ and meditation on his sufferings were central to English Christianity, then and much later. This ardent devotion led to the cultus of the Five Wounds, the Sacred Heart and the Precious Blood; it made Ashridge a centre of pilgrimage; and perhaps its most fervent expression is in the verse of Isaac Watts' noble hymn 'When I survey' which most hymn books now omit:

> 'His dying crimson, like a robe
> Spreads o'er His Body on the tree;
> Then am I dead to all the globe,
> And all the globe is dead to me.'

Thomas Harding already judged himself dead to this world through the Cross. He was a lonely old man; he had continued steadfastly in his faith for the past 20 years, and had no wish to avoid that death on which the Bishop seem determined. He therefore let the Bishop's chaplains say what they would by way of rebuke. But it was on his conscience that he had conformed to many customs such as the use of holy water and receiving holy bread (this does not refer to the Eucharist) not believing that it was otherwise than as God blesses all created things. He had followed Bishop Smyth's advice to the 'known men' when he 'sent them home again, bidding that they should live among their neighbours as good Christian men should do!'. There is an obvious echo of this in the record.

Thomas Harding and the Lord's Supper

Harding's admissions led to another line of questioning: did he regard the Eucharist itself in the same way? Harding argued that at the Last Supper Christ did not give His natural body to the Twelve. He gave them bread which was clearly not identical with the material flesh, born of Mary, which the disciples could see and touch. One can see that both Harding and his interrogators were on the wrong lines. The question is not what

Christ's body was then, but rather what it is now, when He has returned to the throne in Heaven, and his flesh and blood are spirit and life. By the Resurrection, Christ's natural body was transformed into a spiritual body, and His presence in the Lord's Supper is after the manner proper to a spirit.

It was a popular belief that in the Eucharist there is a special condescension of Christ, in which He humbles Himself still more than in the Incarnation; and that though Christ dwells in Heaven, He visits on earth. Again Isaac Watts expresses this belief:

> 'Down from the palace of the skies
> Hither the King descends;'

or again, in a verse of 'Jesus invites His saints' which is now usually omitted:

> 'Amazing favour! matchless grace
> Of our descending God!'

Against this the Lollards held (surely rightly) that there can be no change in the glorified Christ, but only in us and our gifts. Harding said that he had not read that after the Ascension Christ had descended again, but that He remains continually in Heaven. He had held these views for seven years or more, that is since 1525; but he was a man of few words, and gave no clue to what may have happened then.

During the third day of his examination Harding obviously knew that his fate was sealed. He confessed further that he had gone to confession only out of custom and worldly fear, believing all the time that it was right to confess his sins to God alone, and that the faith which he had in God was sufficient for his salvation. His final statement was that he did not believe that the Disciples consumed the natural body of Christ in the Last Supper, but rather bread; and the Bishop did not reply, as he should have done, that the Resurrection has changed everything.

Thomas Harding in Prison

Thomas Harding is said to have been confined for some time in the Bishop's prison at Wooburn called Little-ease, no doubt with hunger and pain enough. Foxe seems to be wrong in saying that he was brought before the Bishop of Lincoln again, but we can accept Foxe's assertion that the execution, fixed for Ascension eve, was postponed for three weeks. Harding was brought back to Chesham on Monday, 28th May, and it was probably that night which he spent in the Parvise, before his formal trial and sentence on Tuesday. The Vicar-General sat under a special commission, together with the Abbot of Thame as Suffragan Bishop and the Rector of Ashridge College. Rowland Messenger, Vicar of High Wycombe, was present, with the two vicars of Chesham and other clergy and gentry, but he did not play the leading part which Foxe assigns to him. If his sermon in fact maintained the jurisdiction of the Bishop of Rome, it was a gesture of defiance; for Convocation had already submitted to the King's will, More had resigned and the die was cast. In any event the Supremacy had played no overt part in the proceedings at the Old Temple.

Thomas Harding Sentenced and Absolved

Dr Rayne read over the record of the examination before Bishop Longland and asked Harding whether he could allege any reasonable cause why the sentence of relapse should not be carried out. Harding seems to have remained silent, and the Vicar-General then promulgated the sentence and relinquished him to the secular power, represented by the King's serjeant.

It was not until then that Harding asked for absolution 'on account of the love of God'. Almost certainly he recalled St Paul's saying that if he gave his body to be burnt, but had no love, it would not profit him. Dr Rayne was apparently expecting this request and immediately granted it, so that Harding could receive the last sacraments. He spent his last night not in church but in a man's house in prayer and meditation, no doubt on the Passion. A strong tradition identifies this house with no.60 in the Broadway; until 1870 this was an old house lying back from the highway, with the infant Chess running in front of it. The site was later occupied by a brush factory, and then by The Carlton Press; access to it can now be obtained by Sills Yard.

The Death of Thomas Harding

Next day, Wednesday, about ten o'clock, Harding came out carrying a little wooden cross (not a crucifix) and was escorted along the High Street and up White Hill by a company with bills and staves. Even this detail does not lack confirmation. The Muster Certificate of 1522 shows that in the Town there were 25 bills, of which 3 were 'good bills', with 10 others in Waterside (one 'good'). Harding himself then owned no weapon. Fire was kindled at a smithy by Waggon Yard.

The 'dell going to Botley at the north end of the town of Chesham' is precisely located by tradition; originally a small chalk-pit by the roadside for marling Dungrove field, it may have given White Hill its name. It was a statutory requirement that heretics should be burnt on a high place before the people, and the traditional site is prominent enough. The tradition that Harding said 'Shall I mount?' is quite credible, and does not imply any doubt or hesitation on his part; it simply means 'are you ready?' and is the kind of small detail which would be remembered.

There is also no reason to doubt Foxe's statement, based on the written testimony of certain inhabitants of Amersham a generation later, that when Thomas Harding was chained to the stake he desired the people to pray for him, forgave his enemies and commended his soul to God, lifting up his hands to heaven and saying 'Jesus, receive my spirit'. But he was not to suffer death by fire. As soon as the fire was lit, someone threw a billet at him and dashed out his brains. Technically, it would seem that he died while awaiting execution. He had not recanted, and it does not appear that he had ever been asked to recant, though his asking for the benefit of absolution may have been so regarded. It was not clear then, and cannot be known now, whether the billet was aimed deliberately (which, however charitably intended, would legally have been murder) or whether it was only meant to earn 40 days' indulgence by bringing a faggot to the stake.

Since Thomas Harding died in good standing, Rowland Messenger's words to the crowd were quite natural and appropriate. 'Good people! When ye come home, do not say that you have been at the burning of a heretic, but of a true Christian man'. After dinner the priests present went to evensong, because it was Corpus Christi even, 'where they fell to singing and chanting with ringing and piping of the organs'. The first mention of an organ at St Mary's was in 1504; the word 'organs' does not imply more than one instrument. On 8th December 1532, the court baron of Chesham Higham (the principal manor of Chesham) recorded the burning of Thomas Harding. The jury did not know what goods he had, or of what value; the bailiff was instructed to take his estate in hand and account for it to the lord of the manor, John de Vere, Earl of Oxford.

The Last of the Lollard Martyrs

W.H. Summers pointed out ('The Lollards of the Chiltern Hills', p.157) that it was Corpus Christi day in 1382 that Philip Repingdon preached the sermon at Oxford which led Archbishop Courtenay to take the first repressive measures against Lollardy, and that the persecution ended just 150 years later with the burning of Thomas Harding, the last martyr of purely Lollard training and sympathies; though it is now clear that in the last years of his life Lollardy in the Chilterns was coming under the influence of the Continental Reformers. It would, nevertheless, be inexact to describe Harding as a Protestant. He died for causes on which all Christians now agree; for liberty of conscience, for reliance on Christ alone for salvation, and for the right and duty to read the Scriptures with understanding, and therefore in the vernacular. All denominations in Chesham have some claim to him. He lived and died in communion with the undivided Western Church, while rejecting its corruptions. In the next generation, under the Elizabethan settlement, he was claimed as a martyr for the Church of England, a claim which the Reformed Churches thought less than justified. In the next century the General Baptists in Buckinghamshire called the Lollards 'our worthy and famous antients'; many of them rejoiced in their Lollard ancestry, as indeed did some early Quakers of this district. Direct or collateral descent from Thomas Harding is still recalled with legitimate pride. It is thus appropriate that the Town of Chesham should join in commemorating the 450th anniversary of the martyrdom of Thomas Harding, a good man who lived among us for ten years and took his death most patiently and quietly, being of the age of sixty years and above.

ooooo0000ooooo

BIBLOGRAPHY

ASTON, MARGARET: 'Lollardy and the Reformation, Survival or Revival?' *History,* June 1964

ASTON, MARGARET: 'Lollardy and Sedition, 1381-1431' in *Peasants, Knights & Heretics,* edited by R.H. Hilton, C.U.P. 1976

ASTON, MARGARET: 'Lollardy and Literacy', *Histor,y* 62, No. 206, October 1977

ASTON, MARGARET: 'Lollard Women Priests?', *Journal of Ecclesiastical History* 31, No.4, October 1980

Ed: ASTON, MARGARET AND COLIN RICHMOND: *'Lollardy and the Gentry* in the *Later Middle Ages'*, Sutton, 1997

BETTENSON, H., ed.: *Documents of the Christian Church,* O.U.P., 1967

BROWN, PETER: *Augustine of Hippo,* Faber, 1967

CHADWICK, HENRY: *The Early Church,* Pelican, 1967

CHADWICK, OWEN: *The Reformation,* Pelican, 1964

COHN, NORMAN: *Europe's Inner Demon,* Paladin, 1975

CROSS, CLARE: *Church and People 1450–1660,* Fontana, 1964

DAVIES, C.S.L.: *Peace, Print & Protestantism 1450–1558,* Paladin, 1977

DEANESLY, MARGARET: *The Lollard Bible,* C.U.P., 1966

DICKENS, A.G.: *The English Reformation, Fontana, 1964*

DICKENS, A.G. & CARR, DOROTHY: *The Reformation in England,* Arnold, 1967

DAVIS, R.G.: *Lollardy and Locality,* Trans. Royal Historical Society, 1999

DOBSON, R.B., ed: *The Peasants' Revolt of 1381,* MacMillan, 1970

FOXE, JOHN: *Acts and Monuments*, Vol.4 ed. Pratt, 1877

FROISSART: *Chronicles,* Penguin, 1968

FRYDE, E.B.: *The Great Revolt of 1381,* Historical Association, 1981

HAMILTON, B.: *The Albigensian Crusade,* Historical Association, 1974

HAY, DENYS: *Europe in the 14th and 15th Centuries,* Longmans, 1966

HEER, F.: *The Medieval World,* Cardinal, 1974

HILL, CHRISTOPHER: *'From Lollards to Leveller'* in *Rebels & Their Causes* edited by M. Cornforth, Laurence & Wishart, 1978

HOLMES, GEORGE: *The Later Middle Ages 1272–1485,* Cardinal, 1974

HUTCHINSON, HAROLD: *The Hollow Crown,* Eyre & Spottiswode, 1961

KNOWLES, DAVID: *The Religious Orders in England: Vol.1,* C.U.P., 1948

LANDER, J.R.; *Government & Community in England 1450–1509,* Arnold, 1980

LEFF, GORDON: *Heresy in the Later Middle Ages, 2 vols,* Manchester U.P., 1967

LEFF, GORDON: *Medieval Thought,* Penguin, 1958

LEFF, GORDON: *John Wycliff, the path to Dissent,* Proc. British Academy 52,
  1966

MCFARLANE, K.B.: *Lancastrian Kings and Lollard Knights,* O.U.P., 1972

MCFARLANE, K.B.: *Wyclif and English Non-Conformity,* Pelican, 1972

MOORE, R.I.: *The Birth of Popular Heresy,* Arnold, 1975

SMITH, S.N.: Cheyne of Drayton Beauchamp, *(typed article, no date)*

SOUTHERN, R.W.: *Western Society and the Church in the Middle Ages,* Pelican,
  1970

SUMMERS, W: *The Lollards of the Chiltern Hill, Kessinger, 2009s*

THOMPSON, A. HAMILTON: *Leicester Abbey,* Backus, 1949

THOMSON, J.A.K.: *The Later Lollards 1414-1520,* O.U.P., 1965

ULLMAN, WALTER: *A Short History of the Papacy in the Middle Ages,* Methuen
  1972

VICTORIA COUNTY HISTORY OF BUCKS, 1, Chapter on Ecclesiastical History

WILKINSON, B.: *The Later Middle Ages in England 1216–1485,* Longmans, 1969

WORKMAN, H.B.: *John Wyclif, 2 vols.,* Oxford, 1926

Unpublished

Register of Bishop Longland (Lincoln) fos. 228 & 228v. Transcript and translation used by kind permission of Miss Frances Burrows.

Acknowledgements
The authors wish to acknowledge the help given by Mrs Anne Thomas, the staff of Chesham Library, and Miss Frances Burrows.

ABOUT THE AUTHORS

The late Dr Arnold Baines was born in Chesham and educated, first at Whitehill School, then at Dr Challoner's Grammar School, before going up to Cambridge to read Mathematics. To complete his studies he went on to read Law. His career was to take him into the Civil Service, to The Ministry of Agriculture, Fisheries & Food, where he rose to become Chief Statistician, and where he remained until his retirement.

From 1953 he was active in Chesham Council, becoming Chairman in 1960-61 and 1970-71, and then Mayor of the newly formed Town Council. He was also a long-standing Member of Bucks County Council.

For Arnold was a Chesham man to his core and its history was his abiding interest. He was also proud of his County and researched both of these tirelessly. This was recognised by the Society of Antiquaries and the Royal Historical Society. At various times he was to hold the Chair of the Buckinghamshire Archaeological Society and the Chiltern Society, and he was a Trustee of the County Museum as well as the Bucks Historic Churches Trust. He was also a Trustee of Trinity Church and involved in several local charities.

In later years he obtained a Doctorate from the Open University. His death, in 2001, robbed Chesham of its dedicated historian.

It was in 1955 that Shirley Foxell came to live in Chesham. A librarian by training, she was also interested in history, and was to become increasingly involved in the local historical scene, joining, in its early days, the Records Group of Chess Valley Archaeological & Historical Society, which took up the ongoing task, begun by the late J.W. Garrett-Pegge, of transcribing Chesham's Parish Registers.

In later years she obtained Degrees from London University – a B.A. in Religious Studies from Goldsmith's College, followed by an M.A. in Church History from King's College. And latterly the ongoing support given by membership of Buckinghamshire's Archaeological & Historical and Record Societies have provided much encouragement. For the story of Chesham's long, complex and sometimes tragic past, coupled with that of its ancient Church, have provided rich sources for study.

This present publication is but one of several projects on which, over the years, she was to work as part of a team in collaboration with Dr Baines. These were to include – as well as this Thomas Harding project - The Lady Elgiva project, the Chesham Town Museum Project, and The Francis Trust.